D0578909

DISCARD

EXTREME SPORTS

SKATEBOARDING
STREET STYLE

BY THOMAS K. ADAMSON

EPIC

BELLWETHER MEDIA • MINNEAPOLIS, MN

EPIC BOOKS are no ordinary books. They burst with intense action, high-speed heroics, and shadows of the unknown. Are you ready for an Epic adventure?

This edition first published in 2016 by Bellwether Media, Inc.

No part of this publication may be reproduced in whole or in part without written permission of the publisher. For information regarding permission, write to Bellwether Media, Inc., Attention: Permissions Department, 5357 Penn Avenue South, Minneapolis, MN 55419.

Library of Congress Cataloging-in-Publication Data

Adamson, Thomas K., 1970-
  Skateboarding Street Style / by Thomas K. Adamson.
    pages cm. – (Epic: Extreme Sports)
  Summary: "Engaging images accompany information about skateboarding street style. The combination of high-interest subject matter and light text is intended for students in grades 2 through 7"– Provided by publisher.
  Audience: Ages 7 to 12
  Includes bibliographical references and index.
  ISBN 978-1-62617-277-7 (hardcover: alk. paper)
  1. Skateboarding–Juvenile literature. 2. Extreme sports–Juvenile literature. 3. ESPN X-Games–Juvenile literature. I. Title.
  GV859.8.A43 2016
  796.22–dc23

                        2015004247

Text copyright © 2016 by Bellwether Media, Inc. EPIC and associated logos are trademarks and/or registered trademarks of Bellwether Media, Inc. SCHOLASTIC, CHILDREN'S PRESS, and associated logos are trademarks and/or registered trademarks of Scholastic Inc.

Printed in the United States of America, North Mankato, MN.

TABLE OF CONTENTS

WARNING
The tricks shown in this book are performed by professionals. Always wear a helmet and other safety gear when you are on a skateboard.

GOLD MEDAL RUN

Nyjah Huston skates to a stair rail. He begins his run with a grind. He skates to another rail. He turns in the air before landing a noseslide. He makes every trick look easy. The crowd cheers his nearly perfect run.

PROTECT YOUR HEAD!

Professionals often wear hats during street style events. However, helmets are strongly recommended.

5

Huston then skates to another stair rail. He pops his board off the ground. He turns and slides down the rail backwards. He **stomps** the landing. This Nollie 270 Lipslide seals the deal. Huston wins the 2014 X Games Skateboard Street gold medal!

BEAT THAT SCORE

Huston's 2014 win was his 5th X Games gold medal. His score was the highest ever at an X Games Skateboard Street final!

SKATEBOARDING
STREET STYLE

In street style skateboarding, skaters do tricks on stairs, rails, and other obstacles. They use objects they would see while skating on the street.

Street skaters do not go for big air. They try to do hard tricks. They invent creative new moves.

SKATEBOARDING STREET STYLE TERMS

Nollie 270 Lipslide—a trick in which the skater jumps and spins almost all the way around before sliding on a rail and then landing straight

noseslide—a trick in which the skater slides using the front of the skateboard

rail—a metal pipe or tube

stair rail—a metal pipe or tube on a set of stairs

truck—the skateboard's metal piece that holds the wheels to the board

STREET STYLE BEGINNINGS

Before skateboarding competitions, people skated on the street. They did tricks on curbs, walls, and even fire hydrants. The X Games course is set up to look like the early days of street style skateboarding.

TAKING OFF

Some early skaters took pictures and videos of their tricks. Then other skaters copied their moves and tried new tricks.

X Games Skateboard Street course

The first street style skateboarding competition was held in 1983 in California. Then the X Games began in 1995. This popular event spread interest in skateboarding.

15

STREET STYLE GEAR

The X Games does not require safety gear for the Skateboard Street event. But trying new moves is dangerous. All skaters should wear helmets. Knee pads, elbow pads, and wrist guards also protect skaters when they fall.

NICE WHEELS
A skateboard's plastic wheels are tough enough to land tricks on the street without wearing down.

THE COMPETITION

In the X Games, skaters get three runs. Each run lasts 50 seconds. Judges give every run a score. They look for difficulty, style, and **originality**. Only a skater's best score counts.

EVENT SCORING

Each run is scored out of 100 points. Judges look for new tricks. Harder tricks score more points. Skaters can do the same trick as someone else. The trick will score higher if it is done with better style.

LUNCHTIME?
The X Games course has included a picnic table.

The X Games Skateboard Street course changes each year. Different obstacles can be used. Every course has to have a good flow from one obstacle to the next.

INNOVATOR OF THE SPORT

name: **Ryan Sheckler**
birthdate: **December 30, 1989**
hometown: **San Clemente, California**
innovations: **Won the X Games gold medal for Skateboard Street in 2003 at only 13 years old**

GLOSSARY

competitions—events in which people perform tricks to win

course—the series of obstacles skaters do tricks on during a street style skateboarding competition

creative—thinking of new ideas

flow—the ease in which skaters can move from one obstacle to the next on the course

grind—a trick in which the skater slides the skateboard's truck, or both trucks, along an object

obstacles—objects that skaters use for tricks

originality—being new and interesting

run—a turn at competing in an event

stomps—landing squarely on the skateboard after a trick without losing balance

style—the way something is done

trick—a specific move in a skateboarding event

TO LEARN MORE

AT THE LIBRARY

Cain, Patrick G. *Skateboarding Street*. Minneapolis, Minn.: Lerner Publications, 2013.

Craats, Rennay. *Skateboarding*. New York, N.Y.: AV2 by Weigl, 2014.

Labrecque, Ellen. *Cool Board Tricks*. Chicago, Ill.: Raintree, 2013.

ON THE WEB

Learning more about skateboarding street style is as easy as 1, 2, 3.

1. Go to www.factsurfer.com.

2. Enter "skateboarding street style" into the search box.

3. Click the "Surf" button and you will see a list of related web sites.

With factsurfer.com, finding more information is just a click away.

INDEX

The images in this book are reproduced through the courtesy of: Fuse/ Getty Images, front cover, p. 15; Rick Kern/ WireImage/ Getty Images, pp. 4-5; Ezra Shaw/ Getty Images, pp. 6-7, 7; Christian Pondella/ Getty Images, pp. 8, 10; Harry How/ Getty Images, pp. 9, 21; Al Fuchs/ NewSport/ Corbis, p. 11; Jeff Gross/ Getty Images, pp. 12-13; Pymcauig/ Universal Images Group/ Newscom, p. 13; Associated Press, p. 14; Marco Govel, p. 16; Stephen Dunn/ Getty Images, p. 17; Zuma Press/ Alamy, p. 18; SGM/ Zuma Press, p. 19; Joe Scarnici/ Zuma Press, p. 20; Joe Seer, p. 21 (top).